THE · WORLD · AROUND · US
NATURE

JENNIFER COCHRANE

Illustrated by
Graham Allen, Mike Atkinson, Pat Lenander
Bernard Robinson, David Wright

WARWICK PRESS

Published in 1991 by Warwick Press,
387 Park Avenue South, New York, New York, 10016.
First published in 1991 by Kingfisher Books.
Copyright © Grisewood & Dempsey Ltd. 1991.

6 5 4 3 2 1
Printed in Spain

**Library of Congress Cataloging-in-Publication
Data**
Cochrane, Jennifer.
    Nature / Jennifer Cochrane.
        p.   cm. — (The world around us)
    Includes index.
    Summary: Examines how plants and animals have
invaded almost every conceivable habitat on land and
sea, below ground and in the air, and adapted to thrive
there.
    ISBN 0-531-19143-5
    1. Adaptation (Biology)—Juvenile literature.
2. Plants—Adaptation—Juvenile literature.
[1. Adaptation (Biology).] I. Title. II. Series.   91-9194
QH546.C58   1991   CIP
574.5—dc20   AC

Contents

Woodpecker

Squirrel

Field vole

Gnawed roots

Otter

Roe deer

Crossbills gnaw crab apples to eat the seeds at the core.

A herring gull track. The middle toe in the webbed foot is about 2 to 3 inches long.

Tracks and Signs

There are plenty of wild animals around, even in cities. But we seldom see them. Many birds and small animals live in our parks and gardens, and there are far more in the fields and woods. The evidence is there to be found if you know what to look for and where to look.

Things to Look For

A tree can be a home to birds, insects, and small mammals. Sometimes you will see a bird's nest or a squirrel's drey in the branches. In a hole high up in the trunk there may be owls or bats. A family of field voles or dormice might make their grassy nests around the roots.

On the ground, look out for the telltale footprints or droppings of foxes and badgers. If you are lucky, you may find owl pellets. These are little balls made up of the bones and fur of prey — the animals the owl has eaten. Or you may even find the skin of a snake. Snakes shed their outer skins as they grow. If you know where to look and are patient, the secrets of nature are there to be found.

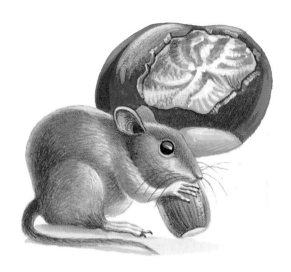

▲ A nut left by a wood mouse shows how the mouse turned it during gnawing.

▲ Adult squirrels make a small hole at the top of a nut before cracking it open.

◀ In its search for insects and grubs, the woodpecker hacks the bark off trees with its beak, leaving clear marks. The squirrel strips the bark to reach the soft layer underneath, which it eats. In winter, the field vole will eat the bark it gnaws off the foot of tree trunks. The roots of young trees are another source of food for the field vole.

The roe deer marks its territory by fraying bark with its antlers. A slide on a snowy or muddy bank may be a sign that otters have been playing there.

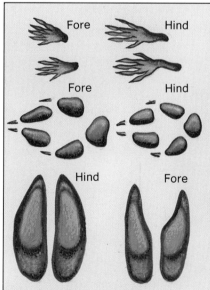

Fore   Hind

Fore   Hind

◀ Tracks made by the tiny shrew show five toes on each foot.

Fore   Hind

◀ The hind-foot of a fox is smaller than the fore-foot. The claws are long.

Hind   Fore

◀ The tracks of the roe deer show the pointed hoofs. The front hoofs are splayed.

Animal Homes

Finding the right place to build a home is very important. A home must be safe and it must be near food. Most animals do not need a real home. They only use nests or dens to shelter their young. The rest of the year they wander in search of food.

A few "social" animals live in large groups, called colonies. Each colony builds a collection of rooms, which may be used for many years. Lemmings, prairie dogs, and rabbits live in such colonies underground.

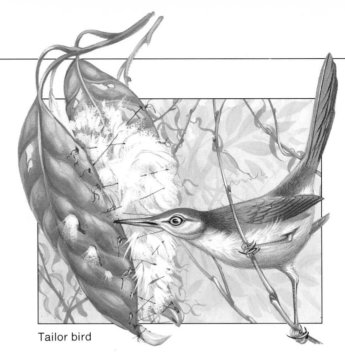
Tailor bird

Traps, Pots, and Nests

An animal may not only build a home to protect its young. Some animals make homes to catch their prey. The trapdoor spider does this. It lies in wait within its camouflaged burrow. When an insect passes, the spider leaps out and pulls it into the burrow. Other animals build homes to store food. The honey pots of the potter wasp are "larder" homes.

Not all birds make nests — the guillemot lays its eggs on a bare rock. But the tailor bird is a skillful nest-builder. It sews leaves together with long plant stems to make a cradle for its eggs.

Trapdoor spider and prey

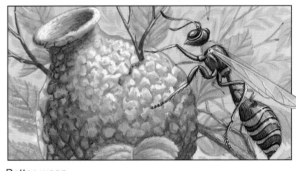
Potter wasp

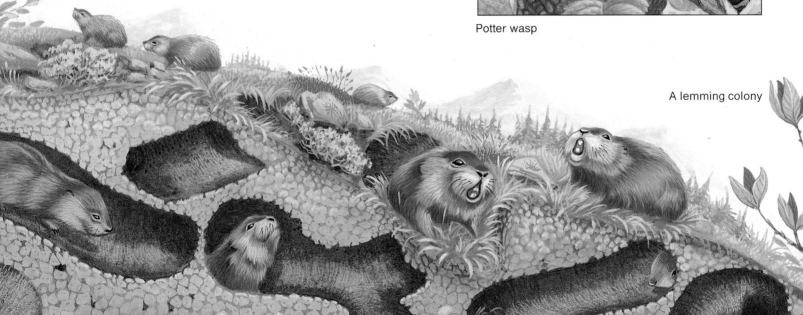
A lemming colony

The Master Builders

The beavers of North America are the master builders of the animal world. They build their island homes, called lodges, on lakes and rivers. Usually they make dams too, to form a pool in which to build their lodge.

Gnawing with their sharp, chisellike teeth, the beavers fell trees. Then they cut the trunks and branches into logs and float them into position. A single dam may need hundreds of tons of wood. The beavers cement the logs together with clay and leaves to make the dam strong.

They build the lodge with the same care. A beaver lodge looks like a mound of sticks and mud. Above the level of the water it may have two or more chambers. All the entrances to the lodge are underwater, so the beavers can come and go in safety when the lake freezes. In the fall they store juicy shoots and bark near the lodge to eat during the long winter. Inside their sturdy home they need not fear hungry predators such as the lynx.

Animal Life Stories

The most important time in an animal's life is its mating and breeding season. Each year, enough young must be produced to replace the animals that have died. In this way the population stays about the same. If a group of animals cannot produce enough young it quickly dwindles and may be in danger of dying out altogether.

Some animals do not need to mate. The tiny amoeba makes its young by simply dividing itself into two. But most animals need both males and females to reproduce. The female produces eggs. Then she mates with a male who fertilizes her eggs with sperm.

Many creatures lay eggs from which their young hatch. Other animals produce only a few eggs inside their bodies and give birth to one or two live young. Many offspring look like their parents when they are born, but some animals go through different stages and forms before they finally become fully developed.

► The amoeba is a tiny water-living animal consisting of only one cell. When the nucleus splits, the whole cell divides to make two amoebae.

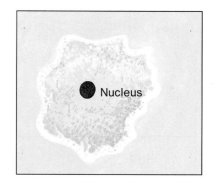

Nucleus

▼ A butterfly egg hatches into a caterpillar. After eating leaves all summer the caterpillar weaves a silk case around itself and becomes a chrysalis. The following spring, a butterfly emerges from the chrysalis.

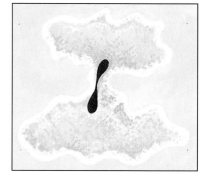

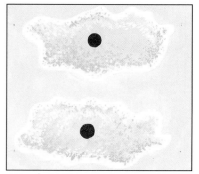

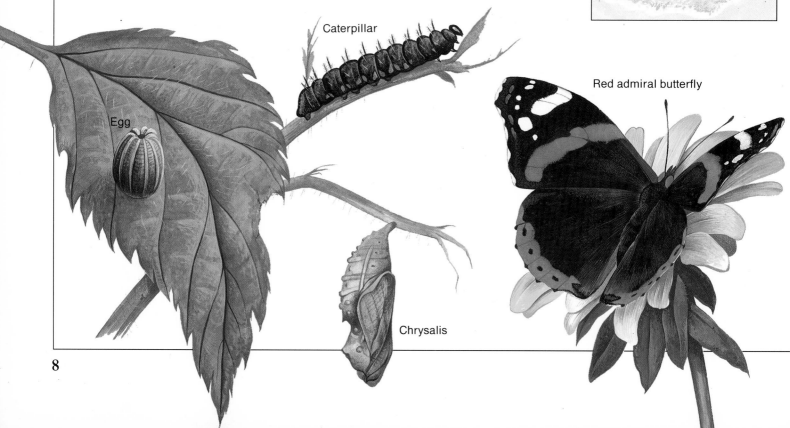

Caterpillar

Egg

Chrysalis

Red admiral butterfly

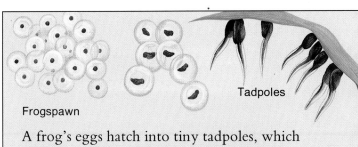

Frogspawn

Tadpoles

Froglet

A frog's eggs hatch into tiny tadpoles, which cling to the leaves of water plants. As they grow they develop back legs, then front legs, then lose their tails and become frogs.

◄Kangaroos are marsupials. They carry their babies in pouches. When a baby is born it crawls into its mother's pouch to feed on her milk. Here it stays, until it is quite large.

▲The sea turtle lays her eggs in a sandy "nest" then leaves them to hatch.

▲When they hatch the babies have to fend for themselves. In danger from hungry birds, they race toward the sea.

Animals and Their Young

Different animals have different ways of ensuring their kind's survival. Some lay so many eggs that there is a good chance of a few young surviving. There is no need for the parents to care for them.

Good Parents

However, there are many excellent parents in the animal world. Birds and mammals have small families, so they take good care of their young. Birds sit on their eggs to hatch them. The parents bring food to the chicks until their feathers have grown and the young birds are able to fly and find their own food.

Only a few mammals, such as cattle, horses, and antelope, have babies that can run about soon after they are born. Many mammal babies are born helpless, often blind and hairless. Their parents must feed and protect them for weeks or months.

▶ When a herring gull chick needs food it pecks at the red spot on the adult's beak. This makes the adult give food to the hungry chick.

Koala bear and baby

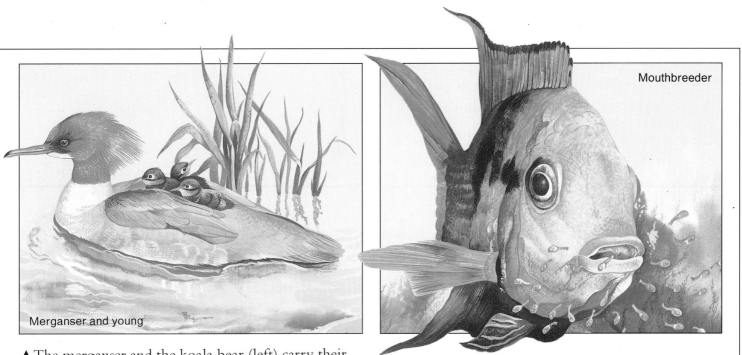

Merganser and young

Mouthbreeder

▲ The merganser and the koala bear (left) carry their babies with them on their backs. Few fish care for their young, but the male mouthbreeder (right) shelters his in his mouth when danger threatens.

▼ A herd of musk oxen works together to protect its young. If they are under attack the adults stand in a circle facing out. The young are safe inside the circle.

11

Food Factories

All animals eat either plants or other animals that feed on plants. But plants are able to make their own food.

Plants take water from the soil and carbon dioxide gas from the air. Then they use the energy in sunlight to change them both into food which helps the plant to grow. This process is called photosynthesis and it takes place mainly in the leaves, which contain chlorophyll, a green chemical. It is chlorophyll that absorbs energy from sunlight. During photosynthesis plants produce a gas called oxygen. Animals need oxygen to breathe, so photosynthesis also helps animals to live.

Support Systems

Roots anchor a plant to the ground. They also absorb water and goodness from the soil. Some types store food. There are two main kinds of root. Fibrous roots are busy systems that often spread deep underground. Tap roots, like the thick root of the carrot, are used to store food.

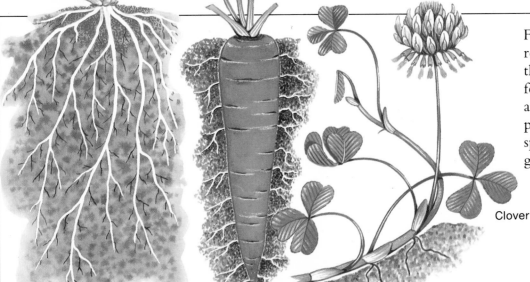

Foxglove

Carrot

Clover

Foxgloves have fibrous roots, while the root of the carrot is a swollen food store. Clover roots anchor and support the plant's stems as they spread along the ground.

▼Most plants grow toward the light and many flowers turn to follow the path of the sun.

▲The sundew is an unusual plant. It gets some of its food by trapping insects and digesting their bodies.

▶Unlike green plants, mushrooms cannot make their own food. They take in food from wood and dead plant matter.

▼A crosssection of a leaf shows the layers of cells inside. Photosynthesis takes place inside these cells and sugary sap is sent from the leaves to the rest of the plant. Carbon dioxide is also taken in through the leaves, and oxygen is given out.

13

New Plants from Old

Most flowers make seeds from which new plants grow. A flower usually needs pollen from another flower of the same kind before it can make seeds. Pollen is sometimes carried from one flower to another by wind, or it can be carried by insects. Attracted by their bright colors, the insects settle on the flowers to search for the sugary liquid called nectar. As they do this, their bodies pick up powdery pollen. When the insect visits the next flower, some of the pollen brushes off and fertilizes the flower so that new seeds can be made.

Scattering the Seeds

Plants cannot move about, so they need help to spread their seeds around. The wind plays an important part in scattering seeds. The seeds of the sycamore, and the downy "parachutes" of thistles and dandelions are all wind-blown.

Animals help seeds to travel, too. Some seeds are hidden inside tasty fruit, and pass through an animal's body after being eaten. Others have tiny hooks or burrs, which catch on to a furry animal's coat and travel with it to other places, far from the parent plants.

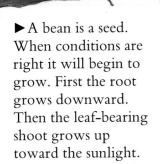

▶ A bean is a seed. When conditions are right it will begin to grow. First the root grows downward. Then the leaf-bearing shoot grows up toward the sunlight.

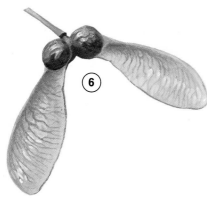

New plant life begins in various ways.

(1) Brightly colored flowers are pollinated by insects, whereas dull colorless flowers, such as grass, are wind-pollinated.

(2) Poppy seeds are carried in a head like a pepperbox. When shaken by the wind the seeds scatter.

(3) Fungi produce spores that are also wind-borne, as are the seeds of reedmaces.

(4) The "parachute" seeds of dandelions,

(5) thistles, and **(6)** the winged sycamore seeds are wind-blown, too. Animals help to disperse some seeds.

(7) Squirrels bury acorns.

(8) A pecking goldfinch may shake plantain seeds off their stalks.

(9) The song thrush may get the gummy seeds of mistletoe berries stuck to its beak while eating them. If the bird wipes these seeds onto another tree, a new plant may grow.

The Balance of Nature

Nothing is wasted in nature. When an animal eats a plant it takes in food from that plant. If the animal is then eaten by another animal, the same food is passed on again. When an animal dies, its body rots — it is broken up by tiny bacteria — and the food and other decaying matter passes into the soil to nourish growing plants.

Links in a Chain

Plants and animals can be grouped together according to what they eat and what, in turn, eats them. These groupings are known as food chains. Food chains can be long and complicated, but a simple chain is shown on the opposite page. Aphids feed on the juices from a rose bush. A ladybug feeds on the aphids and is then caught and eaten by a spider. A hungry shrew makes a meal of the spider. Shrews are hunted and eaten by owls. Each of the animals in the food chain depends in part on the food made in the rose bush.

Some animals feed on things that others pass out in their droppings. Among these is the scarab or dung beetle. It makes a large ball of dung and rolls it away to eat in its burrow.

Sometimes the balance of nature can be upset and a group of animals may outgrow its food supply. If a group of lemmings suddenly increases in number it must migrate in search of food. Many of the lemmings die during the journey, but this means there will now be enough food for those that survive.

▶ When rabbits were introduced into Australia they bred rapidly, turning rich pasture land into desert.

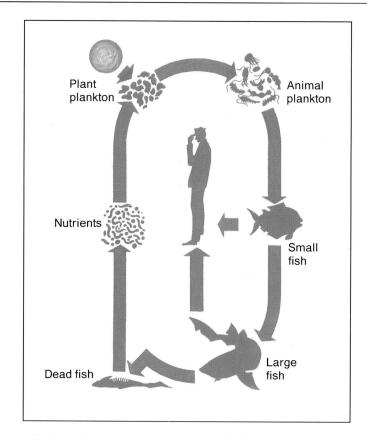

▲ Plant plankton in the sea uses sunlight to make its food. It is eaten by animal plankton, which is food for fish. Some of these fish are eaten by larger fish, others by people. When fish die, their bodies are broken down by bacteria, releasing nutrients which rise to the surface to help feed plankton.

Lemmings

Dung beetle

How Animals Move

All animals move — on land, in water, or through the air. Water animals either float or swim. The water helps to support their bodies. Walking animals need skeletons to hold their bodies upright. Most mammals walk on four legs, only people and apes walk on two legs.

Insects have six legs, spiders have eight, and millipedes many more. Some of these animals can move swiftly. Snakes and worms have no legs at all and pull themselves along the ground. Bats, and most insects and birds also have wings and are able to fly.

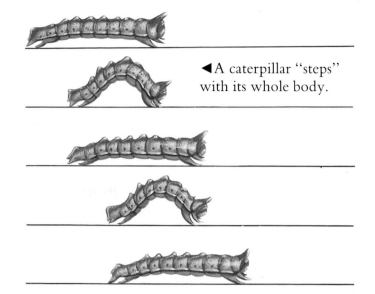

◀A caterpillar "steps" with its whole body.

▶Horses are like most mammals, they need four legs for balance and speed.

▶Most fish flick their strong tails from side to side to drive them through the water. Fins are used for steering.

▶A sidewinder snake uses its whole body to move, but only a small part of it touches the ground at any time.

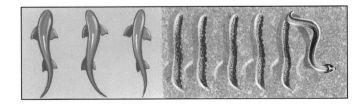

▼When a bird flies, its wings beat the air, keeping it aloft and pushing it along. Some birds also glide, with their wings outstretched.

▶The flying squirrel cannot really fly. It glides from tree to tree, using the skin which stretches between its legs like a parachute.

▼The scallop can swim about by flapping the two halves of its shell together.

▲The hydra is a tiny animal that usually stays in one spot. It moves by doing somersaults on its "arms."

Animal Senses

Many animals have the same senses as we do. As well as sight, hearing, taste, touch, and smell, they have a sense of balance and motion. And they can feel heat and cold, pain, hunger, and thirst. Some animals have only two or three senses, while others have unusual extra ones. Different creatures have developed the senses they need to stay alive.

Suitable Senses

Where an animal lives affects the kind of senses it needs. Cave-dwelling animals do not need good eyesight, but their senses of hearing and touch are well developed. Birds often hunt their

▶ Flies have large eyes made from thousands of lenses. They can see in all directions at once.

▶ A fish's lateral line enables it to "feel" movements in the water around it.

▼ Some fish can surround themselves with an electrical field. They can detect any food or enemies that move within it.

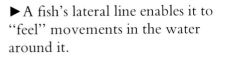

Lateral line

food from the air. They do not need to smell it, but they need good eyesight to spot it.

Extra senses are sometimes used to help a fast-moving animal avoid obstacles even in complete darkness. When a bat is flying around at full speed, its special sense of hearing acts rather like sonar. The bat can pick up echoes of the sounds it makes when they are bounced back by objects in its path.

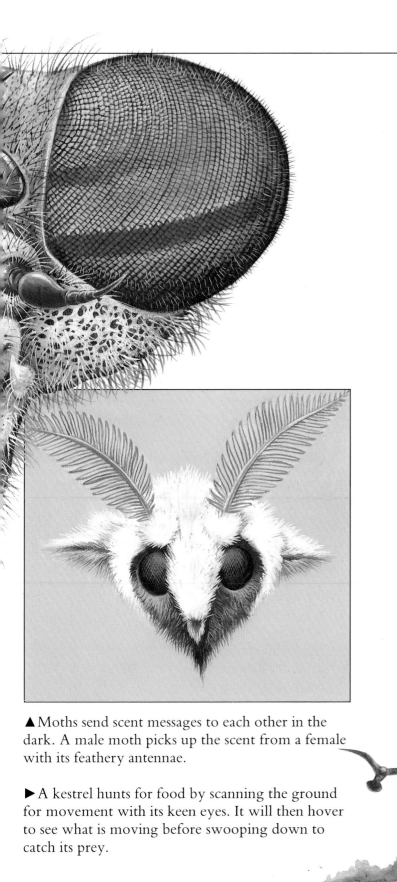

▲A fly's taste organs are on its feet. If it lands on sugar, it will stamp its feet to check that the sugar can be eaten before it begins its meal.

▼Pit vipers are snakes that live in parts of Asia and North America. Their most important sense organs are the tiny pits on each side of their face. These sense heat from the prey's body. So the pit viper can track down a warm-blooded animal in the dark.

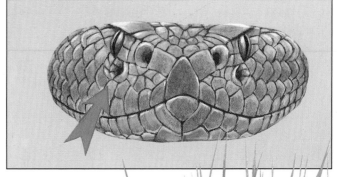

▲Moths send scent messages to each other in the dark. A male moth picks up the scent from a female with its feathery antennae.

▶A kestrel hunts for food by scanning the ground for movement with its keen eyes. It will then hover to see what is moving before swooping down to catch its prey.

Animal Language

Animals use their senses to receive messages. They use language to send out messages of different kinds. A sound or a sign may attract a mate, warn of danger, or indicate the limits of an animal's territory.

Showing Off

An animal language may be a sign language, or one that uses body movements of some kind. The peacock shows off his fine tail before a female bird to let her know that he is ready to mate. Similarly, the pigeon struts around and puffs up his neck feathers.

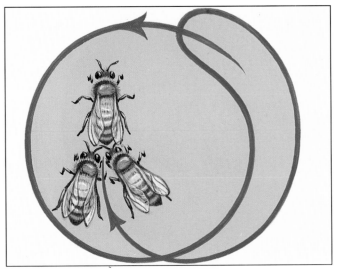

▲ If a bee does a circular dance it means that food can be found nearby.

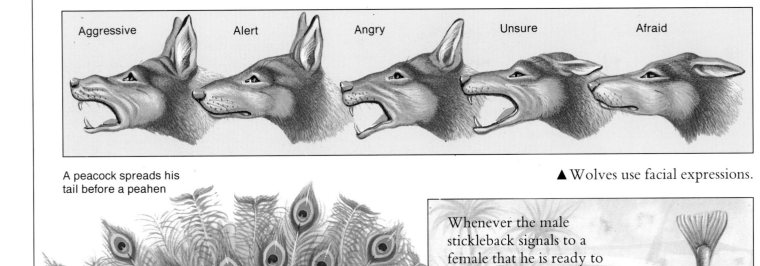

| Aggressive | Alert | Angry | Unsure | Afraid |

A peacock spreads his tail before a peahen

▲ Wolves use facial expressions.

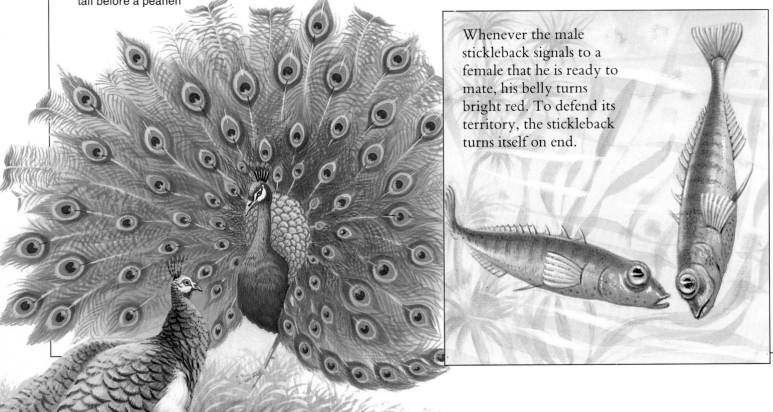

Whenever the male stickleback signals to a female that he is ready to mate, his belly turns bright red. To defend its territory, the stickleback turns itself on end.

The male Adelie penguin will offer a female a pebble. If she takes it, they will build a nest of stones together.

Sound and Movement

Many animal languages use sounds. Dolphins, for example, "talk" in high-pitched squeaks and whistles. Dogs make a lot of different noises — barks, whines, howls, snarls, and so on. But a dog also uses facial expressions and body movements to communicate.

In a beehive, bees communicate by making special dance movements. When a new source of food has been discovered, a bee will do a dance to show the other bees where the food is. In an ant colony, ants communicate with each other by tapping their antennae together.

► When two wolves meet, the weaker one will often cower and sniff at the other's muzzle before lying down to show that he is not a threat.

Animal Adaptations

Every animal is specially adapted, or equipped, to suit the way it lives. Changes in the animal kingdom happen very gradually by a process we call evolution. Slowly, over many millions of years, an enormous number of animals have

▼ The hummingbird's long, slim beak is ideally shaped for probing deep into flowers for nectar.

evolved, or changed, in order to survive in many different environments.

Basic Shapes

Throughout the animal kingdom, certain basic shapes can be found. All insects, for example, have a three-part body — a head, a thorax, and an abdomen. The thorax has three pairs of legs and sometimes wings. All kinds of different insects have evolved from this "standard" insect shape — jumping insects like the grasshopper and the flea, swimming insects like the water boatman, flying insects like butterflies and wasps, and burrowing insects, such as burying beetles.

Fish, birds, and mammals show an amazing range of adaptations, from the first animals that

Winter ptarmigan

Summer ptarmigan

► The giraffe's long neck allows it to reach leaves that are too high for other grazing animals. This gives it an advantage when food is scarce. Because of this, the long-necked giraffes have survived, while the short-necked ones died out long ago.

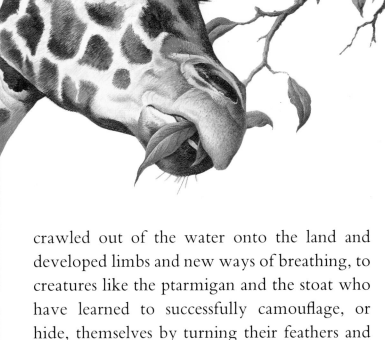

The peppered moth has two forms. The black form has evolved to give better camouflage against smoke-blackened trees.

The Arctic fox of the icy north has tiny ears, which lose little heat.

The desert fox has large ears so that it can lose heat and keep cool.

crawled out of the water onto the land and developed limbs and new ways of breathing, to creatures like the ptarmigan and the stoat who have learned to successfully camouflage, or hide, themselves by turning their feathers and fur white in winter.

Darwin's Finches

Differently-shaped beaks, wings, and feet on birds have all developed to fit various ways of living.

When the naturalist Charles Darwin visited the Galapagos Islands in the Pacific Ocean in 1835, he saw a number of small finchlike birds. Some fed on seeds, others on insects. Each type had a different shape of beak, but Darwin discovered that the birds were closely related. In fact, they were all descended from the "standard" finch, but over millions of years each type of bird had become adapted to eating a different kind of food.

Beaks and Feet

A bird's beak and feet are good clues to its way of life. The woodpecker's hooked claws cling to the bark of trees, while its strong beak hammers into the wood for insects. The warbler's thin, pointed beak is suited to catching small insects. The rail's widespread toes allow it to keep its balance on floating lily leaves.

Reed warbler

Hawfinch

Grouse

Water rail

◄The long-legged avocet probes the mud for food with its slender, curved beak.

Woodpecker

►The eagle's long talons and hooked beak are for holding and tearing its prey.

◄Seed-eating birds like the hawfinch have sturdy beaks with which to crack open hard nuts and seeds.

►The swift catches small insects in flight. It follows them through the air with its wide beak always open.

◄The grouse grows a fringe of feathers around its feet in winter. These act like a pair of snowshoes.

►The crossbill's beak can leaver open pine cones, so that it can take out the seeds with its tongue.

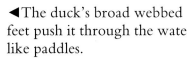

◄The duck's broad webbed feet push it through the water like paddles.

►The flamingo's spoon-shaped beak sifts food from soft mud.

► These insects have all found fairly foolproof ways of hiding themselves.

(1) A katydid conceals itself among lichen.

(2) A purple thorn moth caterpillar mimics a twig on a branch.

(3) The treble bar moth is colored to look just like tree bark.

(4) The cossid moth mimics a tree flower.

(5) When the owlet moth closes its wings it looks like a dead leaf.

(6) The brown speckles on a leaf bug closely resemble the marks on leaves.

(7) Thorn tree hoppers mimic thorns.

(8) Stick insects are almost impossible to see on trees and shrubs.

(9) The orchid mantis mimics a colorful tropical flower.

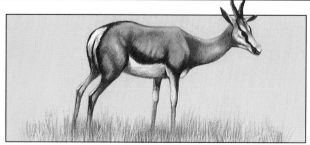

▲ Antelope have dark backs and light bellies to help disguise their shape, making them harder to see among the shadows of the grasses on which they feed.

▲ Flounders cannot swim fast to escape their enemies. Instead, they hide by changing the color of their bodies to match the sandy seabed on which they live.

Animals in Hiding

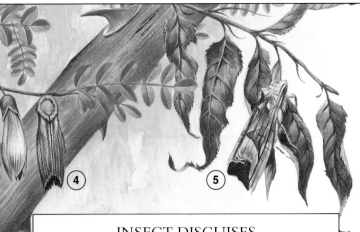

▲ The tiger lives in sunny open grasslands. Its stripes blend in so well with the shadows of trees and tall grasses that smaller animals are unaware of the tiger lying in wait for them.

There are two good reasons why animals find it useful to hide — to avoid being eaten and to catch their own food by lying in wait for unwary victims. Among the most successful players of animal hide-and-seek are those that use either camouflage or mimicry, or a combination of both. Camouflaged animals are colored to match their surroundings. Mimics often look like part of a plant.

Confused by Color

Lots of different animals use camouflage. Grasshoppers and tree snakes are green to match the grasses and leaves around them. Polar bears living in the snowy Arctic are white. The chameleon is a master of disguise. It can even change its color to match its background. Other animals use more complicated patterns. The bold stripes on a zebra confuse an enemy so that it is difficult to see where one zebra in a herd begins and another ends.

Danger all Around

Fish face danger from birds above them and from other fish below. So many of them have dark backs and light-colored bellies. The dark back blends with the surface of the sea, making the fish difficult to spot from the air. From below, the silvery belly blends with the light shining on the water above.

In sunny tropical seas, fish are often brightly patterned. The patterns break up their shapes, making it difficult for their enemies to see them against a background of colorful corals and sponges.

Escape and Defense

The simplest way for some animals to escape from danger is to run faster than their enemies. Many creatures — ostriches, horses, antelope, and others — rely on speed. Most of them have sharp eyes and ears to give them early warning of any predators that are near.

Many small animals hide from danger in their burrows or in the undergrowth. Young ones are often hidden in safe places by their parents until they can fend for themselves. Timid creatures simply "freeze" when danger is at hand. By keeping perfectly still, young deer have a good chance of staying alive. Their coloring acts as camouflage, so they are very difficult to detect unless they move.

True or False?

Some animals are brightly colored to warn hunters that they are poisonous or that they taste nasty. Their bold markings are called "warning colors." Bees and wasps have yellow and black stripes to warn hungry birds that they risk being stung if they attack.

Warning colors provide such a good defense that perfectly harmless animals sometimes copy them. This kind of animal trickery is another form of mimicry.

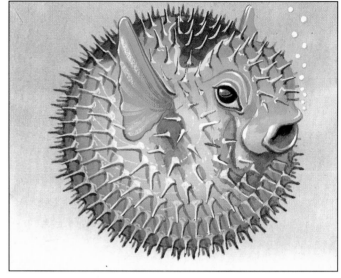

▲ The porcupine or puffer fish blows itself up into a spiky ball to look more frightening.

▲ The skunk defends itself by raising its tail and squirting a vile-smelling fluid at its attackers.

◀ The frilled lizard of Australia can open out a large collar around its neck, making it look bigger and more startling.

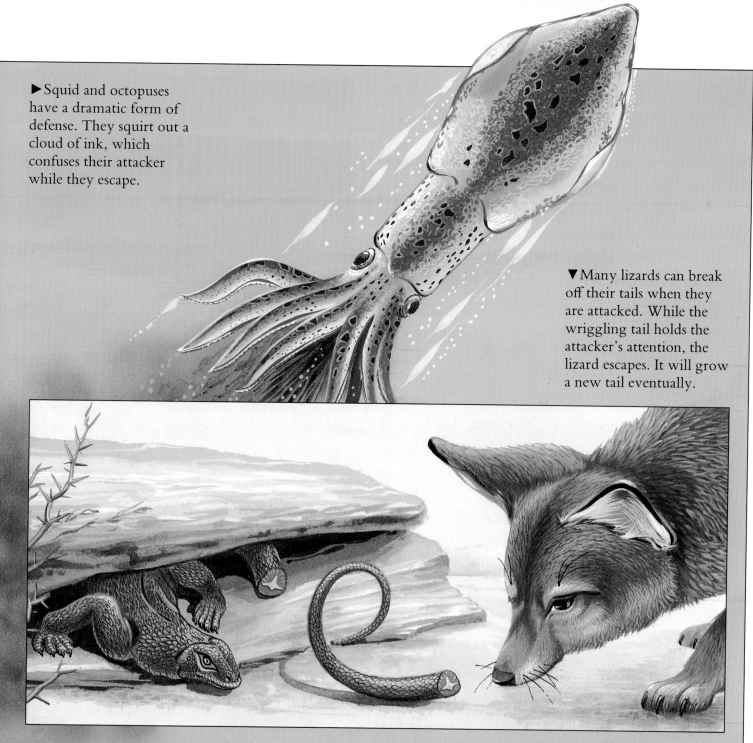

►Squid and octopuses have a dramatic form of defense. They squirt out a cloud of ink, which confuses their attacker while they escape.

▼Many lizards can break off their tails when they are attacked. While the wriggling tail holds the attacker's attention, the lizard escapes. It will grow a new tail eventually.

Pangolin

◄Some animals have a different approach to defense altogether. They simply curl up and stay in one spot. These animals usually carry the protection they need on their backs. Hedgehogs are covered with sharp spines, while pangolins and armadillos both have a covering of overlapping horny scales, similar to a coat of armor. As long as they stay curled up it is difficult for an attacker to get at them. Armadillos also have strong legs and claws and will burrow underground if frightened.

Midnight World

Most animals are active during the day, but at sunset, nocturnal animals emerge and take advantage of less crowded conditions. Many of these nighttime creatures have developed special night senses.

As night falls, rabbits and hedgehogs come out to feed, and foxes and badgers start their night's foraging. Bats and nightjars take to the air in pursuit of moths and other flying insects.

Unlike owls, which use their keen eyes and ears to find their prey, bats have poor eyesight. Instead, they rely on their special sense of hearing, which acts like a form of sonar. Some moths can "jam" the bat's signals. They send out high-pitched squeaks that confuse the bat's echo sounding equipment long enough for the moth to escape.

▲ The strange creatures of the deep sea live in darkness all the time. They make their own light to find mates and to lure prey within reach.

Nightjar

Badgers

Field mouse

►Owls have excellent night vision. Their eyes are in the front of their heads so, unlike most birds, the owl has binocular vision — it can judge distances very accurately. Its eyes can spot any movement and its ears can detect the slightest rustle.

Owls cannot move their eyes, so they have to turn and move their heads to see anything that is not directly in front of them. But the tubular shape of the owl's eye, and its large lens, mean that the owl has sharper vision than we have.

◄Bats use an echo sounding system to locate objects. They make high-pitched sounds that bounce back from obstacles in their path.

Human eye

Lens

Owl's eye

Bat

Fox

Hedgehog

Rabbits

Stoat

Cow seal and pup

Europe

South Africa

Animal Journeys

◄ Hungry wolves keep a close watch on a herd of caribou. They will attack any animal that strays from the safety of the migrating herd.

In their search for food or new breeding grounds, a number of animals make very long journeys called migrations.

By Land and Air

The large herds of wildebeest, giraffes, and antelope that roam the Serengeti plains in Africa, follow the grass as it ripens in the rainy season. They move in a great circle, taking a year to get back to their starting point and breeding as they travel.

The reindeer and caribou of northern countries, journey south in the winter to find food, returning northward in the spring.

Swallows breed in North America and Europe when it is warm. When the days shorten and there are fewer insects to feed on, the swallows fly to South America and South Africa for the southern summer. There they remain, until winter sends them north again.

By Sea

There are ocean wanderers too. Seals migrate long distances across the sea to rocky islands, where they mate and have their pups.

Eels hatch from eggs laid in the Sargasso Sea. From there, they drift across the Atlantic Ocean feeding and growing as they go. When the young eels, or elvers, reach the coasts of Europe and North America, they swim up rivers. After living in fresh water for several years, they make the long journey back to the Sargasso Sea again to mate and then die.

Swallow

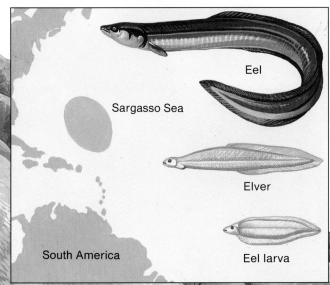

Eel

Sargasso Sea

Elver

South America

Eel larva

Escaping the Cold

In winter, when the days are short and cold, many plants die and there is less food for animals to eat. Some animals escape from the food shortage and the bitter cold by migrating to warmer places, others go to sleep. This winter sleep is called hibernation.

A Long Winter's Night

Before hibernating, an animal stores fat in its body. By the fall, bears have produced thick layers of fat under their skins. They will sleep through the winter in caves. Some fishes bury themselves in the mud at the bottom of ponds and lakes. Toads, tortoises, newts, and snakes hide in crevices in rocks or tree roots. When they wake in spring, they are thin and hungry.

▲ Bats find a dry cave and hibernate while hanging from the roof. If the temperature rises, they will fly out and feed. A bat's temperature may fall so low when it is asleep that dew forms on its fur.

Snake

Stoat

Dormouse

Toad

Tortoise

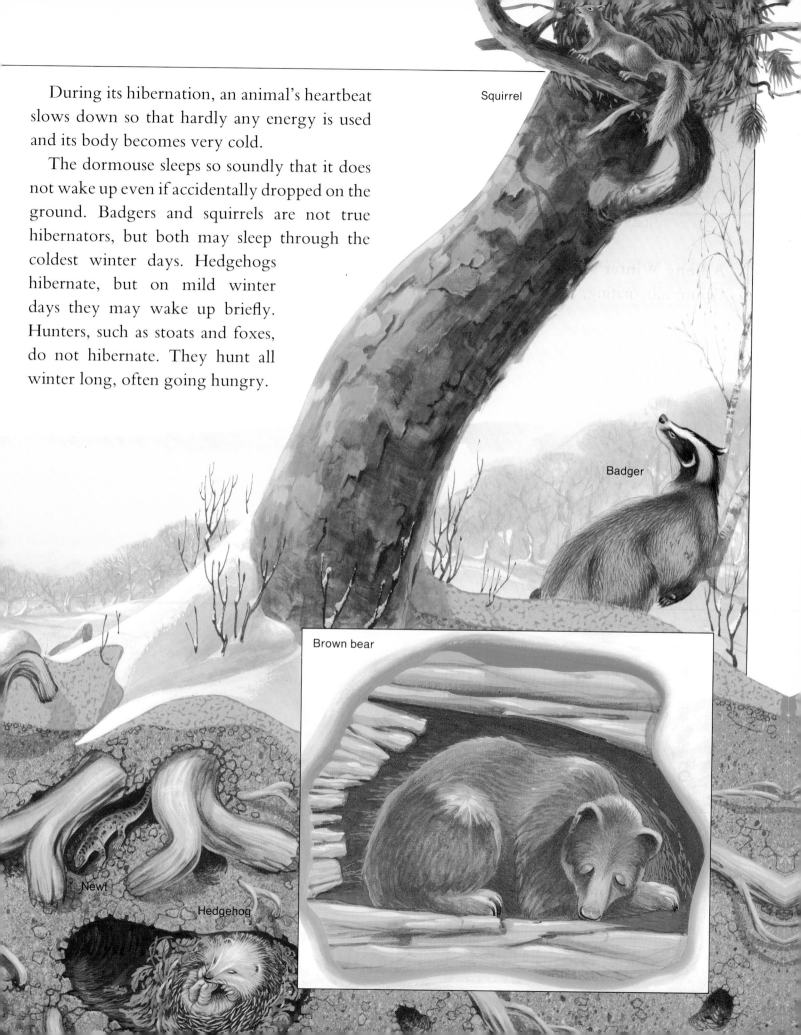

During its hibernation, an animal's heartbeat slows down so that hardly any energy is used and its body becomes very cold.

The dormouse sleeps so soundly that it does not wake up even if accidentally dropped on the ground. Badgers and squirrels are not true hibernators, but both may sleep through the coldest winter days. Hedgehogs hibernate, but on mild winter days they may wake up briefly. Hunters, such as stoats and foxes, do not hibernate. They hunt all winter long, often going hungry.

Squirrel

Badger

Brown bear

Newt

Hedgehog

Animal Partners

Every animal relies on other creatures in some way. Some find safety in numbers. The huge herds of zebras, gazelles, wildebeest, giraffes, and other animals that roam the plains of Africa find it safer to live together. But some animals can find themselves sharing their home with quite different lodgers.

Odd Couples

In New Zealand, the lizardlike tuatara occasionally shares the same cliff-top burrow as the shearwater seabird. While a rattlesnake will sometimes move into a marmot's burrow, and hibernate there for the winter. On the coral reef, the damsel fish makes its home among the stinging tentacles of a sea anemone. Other fish would be stung to death, but the damsel fish is protected by a slimy liquid covering its body. These are not true partnerships, however, because only one partner gains anything from it.

Eagle and starling

◄ Tick birds and cattle egrets ride on the backs of rhinoceroses. At the same time, they eat the tiny insects that settle on the rhino's skin or are disturbed by its feet.

Rattlesnake and marmot

A spur-winged plover, Egyptian plovers and Nile crocodile

Damsel fish

One Good Turn . . .

In a true partnership, both animal partners benefit. They may gain food, shelter, protection from their enemies, or a better chance of breeding successfully.

Starlings may nest very close to the eyrie of a golden eagle. The starlings' enemies are afraid of the larger bird, and the eagle does not mind because the starlings give early warning of any would-be intruders.

An even more remarkable partnership is that of the Egyptian and spur-winged plovers and the Nile crocodile. The plovers regularly walk inside the jaws of the crocodiles — and walk safely out again. They go there to feed on the parasites that live inside crocodiles' mouths.

Parasites are animals that live on other animals and do them harm. In the sea, fish such as the shark and the moray eel are plagued by these pests. Fortunately, there are armies of cleaner fish like the tiny wrasse, which eat the parasites and so keep the larger fish healthy. Even the fiercest fish will allow cleaner fish to swim safely within its mouth.

Insect Communities

A few bees and wasps live alone, and they are known as "solitary" insects, but most are "social" insects, as are ants and termites. They live together in large colonies and are especially successful at organizing the life of their communities. Each individual insect has a job to do, and it relies on the other insects to do their jobs too — on its own, it would soon die.

Inside the Nest

Social insects build large nests. Inside the nests of bees and wasps, the most important insect is the queen. The workers look after the nest and keep it clean. They take care of the eggs and feed the larvae. And they take food to the queen, whose job is to lay eggs and control the life of the colony.

In an ants' nest, there may be more than one queen and a great number of worker ants. Some workers have huge jaws. These are the soldier ants and their job is to defend the colony.

Although termites are not related to ants, they have a similar way of life and are sometimes called white ants. Some termites build huge nests from soil mixed with their own saliva. These nests may be up to 20 feet high.

Some ants burrow underground. Others build mounds of earth with a maze of tunnels inside. Most nests contain a number of chambers or rooms which are used for different purposes. Some rooms house queen ants with their eggs, others are used as nurseries for the young, or as rest rooms for the worker ants.

Life in the Pond

Some of nature's most fascinating secrets can be discovered in a simple pond. Even a small sample of pond water contains an amazing variety of life in miniature. Lots of different tiny creatures live in harmony in a pond. Their community is carefully balanced and, because it is small, it is easy to observe.

Seasonal Changes

Some pond creatures can be found all the year round. Others, like frog tadpoles and the larvae of the mosquito, are there only at certain times of the year. The busiest time in a pond is spring or summer.

Pond animals find it difficult to breathe in the summer. When it is hot the water becomes stagnant and the lack of oxygen in it may kill some of the creatures living there.

In winter, when the water freezes, many pond creatures hibernate by buring themselves in the mud at the bottom of the pond. When the water warms up in spring, they come out and carry on their lives.

From Water to Air

Many insects that spend their adult lives flying about, begin life in a pond or stream. The dragonfly nymph lives underwater for a year or more, feeding and growing. When it is ready, it crawls up a reed stem into the sunlight and turns into an adult insect. But a host of other animals — fish, amphibians such as newts, insects, and crustaceans — spend their whole lives in the pond, feeding on the plants or other tiny creatures that abound there.

▶ All these tiny creatures are found living in and around ponds.
(1) Dragonfly
(2) Water beetle
(3) Pintail
(4) Frog
(5) Pond skater
(6) Caddis fly
(7) Frog spawn
(8) Water beetle
(9) Mosquito larvae
(10) Pond snail
(11) Common newt
(12) Crested newt
(13) Diving beetle
(14) Tadpoles
(15) Stickleback
(16) Diving beetle's air bubble
(17) Water spider
(18) Water boatman
(19) Snail eggs
(20) Ramshorn snail
(21) Caddis larvae

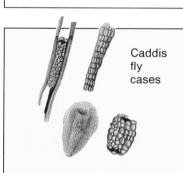

Caddis fly cases

Caddis fly larvae live underwater until fully grown. Some build portable homes, or cases, to live in from twigs, or leaves, or gravel, bound up with silk from their own bodies.

Life on the Seashore

Periwinkle

Serrated wrack

Spider crab

Sea thong

Blenny

Sea lettuce

Tube worm

Dahlia anemone

Hermit crab

Common starfish

Limpets

The seashore is home to a rich variety of plants and animals, although many are faced with difficult living conditions. The region between the high- and low-water marks is particularly changeable. The tide comes in twice a day, so the plants and animals that live here are sometimes covered by salt water, while at other times they are exposed to the hot sun, or cold wind or rain.

The animals that live on the seashore survive when the tide is out by sheltering in rock pools, or by burrowing into the sand. Some, like limpets, whelks, winkles, and barnacles, cling to rocks when the tide recedes. Like crabs, these hard-shelled animals are well protected for life out of the water.

Animals with soft bodies, like the sea slug, fish, and sea anemones, shelter in shallow rock pools at low tide. They can often be found hiding in the crevices among the rocks and boulders. Larger pools may harbor sea urchins or starfish. The starfish has rows of sucker feet on the underside of its arms, which enable it to clamber about the sides of the rocks.

Nature's Blueprints

Young animals and plants normally look like their parents. This is because the female egg and the male sperm or pollen both contain special "blueprints," or patterns, called genes. It is these genes that affect how every living thing looks and functions.

Color Codes

For any one characteristic, such as the color of a flower or the color of an animal's eyes, there will be at least two genes, one from each parent. When any animals or plants reproduce, each parent passes on to their offspring one of the genes from every pair they themselves were born with.

In the diagram below, the parent flower labeled "pure red" has two genes for the color red. The "pure white" parent flower has two genes for white. When one of these flowers fertilizes the other, the crossbred flowers that result will all have one gene for red and one for white. But because the red gene is stronger, all these first generation crossbred flowers are red.

Cross-breeding

When two crossbred plants reproduce, however, a variety of gene combinations will appear among the second generation flowers. Below, the crossbred plants have produced three red flowers and one white flower. On average, one flower in every four will inherit two "red" genes and so will be red. Two other red flowers will each have one "white" and one "red" gene. They are red because the gene for red is stronger. The white flower will have two "white" genes.

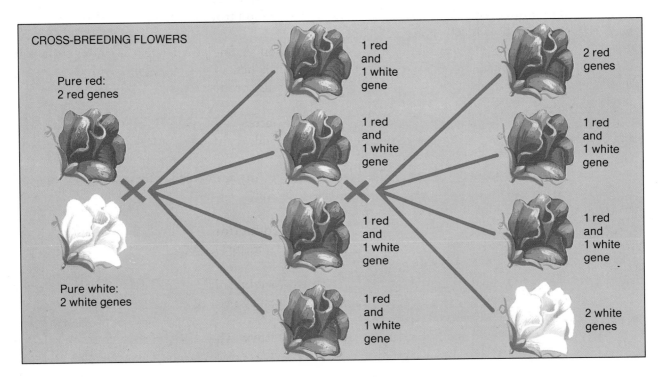

CROSS-BREEDING FLOWERS

Pure red: 2 red genes

Pure white: 2 white genes

1 red and 1 white gene

1 red and 1 white gene

1 red and 1 white gene

1 red and 1 white gene

2 red genes

1 red and 1 white gene

1 red and 1 white gene

2 white genes

Useful Words

Amphibian An animal that can live both on land and in water, for example, frogs and newts. Most amphibians begin life in water.

Bacteria Microscopic living things, more like plants than animals, but related to both. All bacteria consist of only one cell. Some bacteria cause disease, but many are very useful.

Camouflage The color (and sometimes the pattern) of an animal's skin that makes it blend in with its background.

Cell The smallest unit of life, from which all plants and animals are made. A few animals and plants consist of only one cell, but most are made up of millions of cells.

Colony A group of animals of the same kind that live very closely together in the same place.

Crustacean One of the group of multilegged animals that includes shrimps, crabs, and wood-lice. Nearly all crustaceans have a hard outer shell and live in water.

Egg A female cell that will grow into a new young plant or animal, once it has been fertilized by a male sperm or pollen cell.

Evolution The process by which plants and animals gradually change, usually over millions of years, in order to suit their surroundings.

Fertilization The point at which male sperm — or pollen in plants — joins with the female egg to create a new plant or animal.

Hibernation A type of very deep sleep that some animals go into in order to survive the winter cold. During hibernation, animals use very little energy, so they are able to live off the fat they have stored in their bodies in summer.

Larva (plural **larvae**) The young form of some kinds of animal — for example, some insects and fish — when they hatch from their eggs.

Mammal An animal that gives birth to live young and feeds them with milk from its own body. Mammals have warm blood and usually have hair or fur on their bodies.

Marsupial A type of mammal that carries and feeds its young inside a pouch on the mother's body. A kangaroo is a marsupial.

Migration A long journey made at a regular time of year by an animal, usually in search of food or breeding grounds.

Mimicry The shape and coloring of an animal that makes it look like another kind of animal, or a part of a plant.

Nectar Sweet sugary liquid that is produced in the base of a flower.

Nocturnal A nocturnal animal is one that is mainly active at night and sleeps during the day.

Parasite A plant or animal that lives on or inside another and feeds off it.

Photosynthesis The process by which plants make food from sunlight, air, and water.

Pollen A fine powder that contains male plant cells. When a pollen cell joins with a plant's egg cell they produce seeds.

Predator An animal that hunts other animals for food.

Prey Any animal that is hunted by other animals for food.

Reproduction The process by which all living things create new members of their own kind.

Sperm In animals, a male cell that combines with an egg cell to create a new animal.

Territory The area that an animal, or group of animals, considers to be its own.

Index

A
amoebae 8
antelope 28, 30, 35
ants 23, 40–41
armadillos 31
avocets 26

B
bacteria 16–17, 47
badgers 5, 32, 37
bats 5, 20, 32–33, 36
bears 36–37
beavers 7
bees 22, 30, 40
birds 6, 10, 15, 18–19,
    22–23, 24–25, 26–27,
    33, 34, 38–39
breeding 8–11, 46
butterflies 8

C
caddis flies 42
camouflage 25, 28–29, 47
caribou 35
caterpillars 8, 18, 28
chameleons 29
chlorophyll 12
crabs 44–45
crocodiles 39
crossbills 4, 27

D
damsel fish 39
Darwin, Charles 25
deer 4, 5, 30
dogs 22–23
dolphins 23
dormice 5, 36–37
dragonflies 42
ducks 27
dung beetles 16–17

E
eagles 27, 38
eels 35
eggs 8, 40, 47
egrets 38
evolution 24–25, 47
eyes 20, 32–33

F
field voles 4–5
fish 16, 18, 20, 29, 36,
    39
flamingos 27
flies 20–21
flight 18–19
flowers 14–15, 46
flying squirrels 19
food chains 16–17
foxes 5, 25, 32–33, 37
frilled lizards 30
frogs 9, 42
fungi 15

G
gazelles 38
giraffes 25, 35, 38
grasshoppers 29
grouse 26–27
guillemots 6

H
hawfinches 26–27
hedgehogs 31, 32–33, 37,
herring gulls 4, 10
hibernation 36–37, 47
horses 18
hummingbirds 24
hydra 19

I
insects 18, 24, 28–29,
    40–41

K
kangaroos 9
kestrels 21
koala bears 10–11

L
lemmings 6, 16–17
lizards 31

M
mammals 10, 47
marmots 38–39
marsupials 9, 47
mergansers 11

mice 5, 32
migration 34–35, 47
millipedes 18
mimicry 29, 30, 47
moths 21, 25, 28, 32
movement 18–19
mushrooms 13
musk oxen 11

N
nests 6, 40–41
newts 36–37, 43
nightjars 32
nocturnal animals 32–33,
    47

O
octopuses 31
otters 4–5
owls 5, 32–33

P
pangolins 31
parasites 39, 47
peacocks 22
penguins 23
photosynthesis 12–13, 47
pigeons 22
pit vipers 21
plaice 28
plankton 16
plants 12–15, 46
plovers 39
polar bears 29
pollen 14, 47
ponds 42–43
porcupine fish 30
potter wasps 6
prairie dogs 6
ptarmigan 24–25

R
rabbits 6, 16, 32–33
rattlesnakes 38–39
reed warblers 26
reindeer 35
rhinoceroses 38
roe deer 4–5
roots 12

S
scallops 19
sea anemones 39, 45
seals 34–35
seashores 44–45
seeds 14–15
senses 20–21
shearwaters 38
shrews 5
skunks 30
snakes 5, 18, 29, 36
sounds 22–23
spiders 6, 18
squid 31
squirrels 4–5, 15, 37
starfish 45
starlings 38
sticklebacks 22, 43
stoats 25, 36
sundews 13
swallows 34–35
swifts 27

T
tadpoles 9, 42
tailor birds 6
termites 40
tick birds 38
tigers 29
toads 36
tortoises 36
tracks 4–5
trapdoor spiders 6
trees 5
tuataras 38
turtles 9

W
wasps 30, 40
water rails 26
wildebeest 35, 38
wings 18
winter 36–37
wolves 23, 34–35
wood mice 5
woodpeckers 4–5, 26–27

Z
zebras 28, 38